STRONG WOMEN JOURNAL

STRONG WOMEN
journal

MOTIVATING PROMPTS,
EXERCISES, AND AFFIRMATIONS
TO EMPOWER YOUR TRUE SELF

Jessica Thiefels

ROCKRIDGE
PRESS

For general information on our other products and services or to obtain technical support, please contact our Customer Care Department within the United States at (866) 744-2665, or outside the United States at (510) 253-0500.

Rockridge Press publishes its books in a variety of electronic and print formats. Some content that appears in print may not be available in electronic books, and vice versa.

Interior and Cover Designer: Jami Spittler
Art Producer: Alyssa Williams
Editor: Olivia Bartz
Production Editor: Rachel Taenzler
Production Manager: Riley Hoffman

Illustrations © DivinHX/Shutterstock, cover and pp. II, VI, 156; Curly Pat/Creative Market, pp. V, X, 2, 21, 22, 24, 44, 46, 65, 66, 68, 87, 88, 90, 109, 110, 112, 131, 132, 134, 154.

Paperback ISBN: 978-1-68539-019-8
R0

THIS JOURNAL
BELONGS TO

....

CONTENTS

INTRODUCTION

I have the word "strength" tattooed in Gaelic on my hip. It's also tattooed in my tissue, stitched into the fabric of my life. In short, I was born to write this journal for you.

I first knew the power of strength when I was two years old and my mother walked away from my father, who was more concerned about drinking than being a dad. She had to take care of a baby while healing herself and working a full-time job to pay the bills. From that point on, strength became my default, whether I was dealing with bullies in eighth grade or taking a big risk and moving across the country in my early twenties.

What you'll discover in this journal, as I've learned in my experiences, is that strength is not defined by a single characteristic. Strength requires both grit and vulnerability. It can look like crying hard and accepting the worst or doing the impossible and pushing ahead when you'd rather walk away.

Strength is cultivated during challenging life situations when moving forward requires being strong. However, it can also be developed through intentional practices, such as the ones you'll find in this journal.

On these pages, you'll discover affirmations, exercises, journal prompts, and practices that help you build strength. All of them come from my own experiences of being strong and helping my clients and community build strength, too.

Although this journal is a supportive resource, any ongoing or debilitating feelings of depression or anxiety should be addressed by a medical professional. You can find a therapist, psychologist, or counselor at PsychologyToday.com/us/therapists. You can also contact your health insurance provider, who can direct you to people and resources covered by your insurance.

As you dive into this journal, remember that your strength is as multidimensional as you are. Use these exercises, practices, affirmations, and prompts to recognize the many ways you're already strong and the strength you have yet to discover.

How to Use THIS BOOK

In this journal, you'll find seven sections, each meant to help you cultivate and affirm different aspects of your strength. Within each section are four elements:

- **EMPOWERING AFFIRMATIONS**

- **INSIGHTFUL JOURNAL PROMPTS**

- **EXERCISES TO BE DONE WITHIN THE JOURNAL**

- **PRACTICES TO BE DONE OUTSIDE THE JOURNAL**

You can complete each section from start to finish, or you can flip through the pages to pick and choose what you want to focus on. Before diving in, however, I recommend starting with section 1. In section 1, you will discover your own definition of strength and tap into what it means to you personally. Setting this foundation will help you get the most out of your journal.

Once completed, you can page through to find what you need when you need it, whether that's an empowering affirmation or a strength-building practice. You can use this journal on days when you need a reminder of your strength, as a part of your regular morning routine, or simply when you want to take some time to focus on yourself.

There's no "right" way to use this journal. Let it empower and guide you in whatever way feels most supportive.

TAP INTO WHAT BEING A STRONG WOMAN MEANS TO YOU

YOU HAVE LIKELY SEEN movies or read books about strong women who are fighting for what they believe in or overcoming seemingly impossible physical feats. This is just one aspect of strength. A woman accepting, knowing that the only option she has left is to walk away—that's strength. A woman asking for help when she can no longer do it on her own—that's strength.

In this section, you're going to explore what being a strong woman means to you and tap into the strength that's already inside of you. Even if you've picked up this journal because you want to cultivate strength, I assure you, you're already stronger than you think.

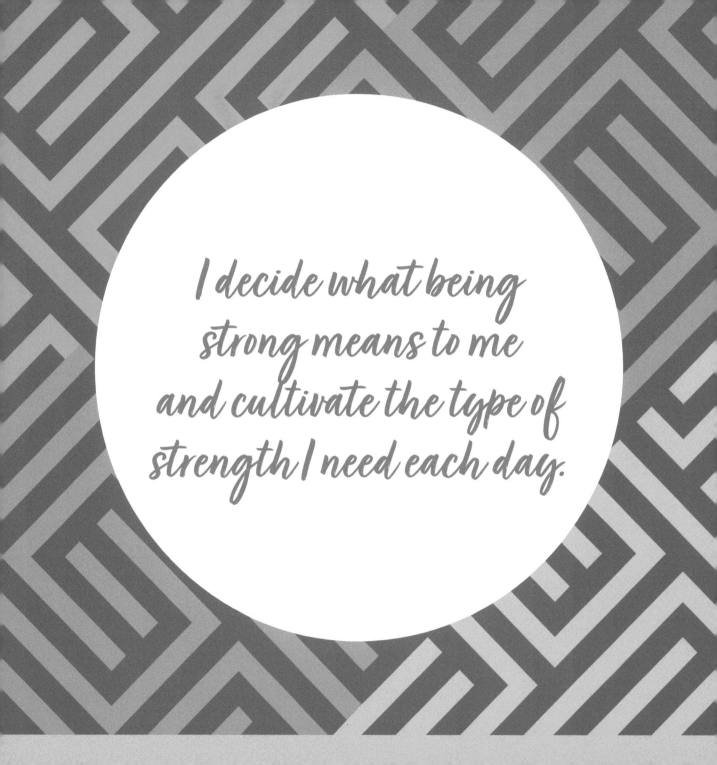

I decide what being strong means to me and cultivate the type of strength I need each day.

What is your definition of "a strong woman"? You can make a list of words and phrases or write down the definition in paragraph style. How close are you to being this strong woman? What do you need to work on most to become her?

_____

_____

_____

_____

_____

_____

_____

_____

_____

_____

_____

_____

_____

_____

_____

_____

_____

_____

TAP INTO WHAT BEING A STRONG WOMAN MEANS TO YOU

When you look back on your life, which woman or women modeled strength the most to you? Describe a time when you experienced their strength and explain any lessons you learned that can be used in your life now.

_____

_____

_____

_____

_____

_____

_____

_____

_____

_____

_____

_____

_____

_____

_____

_____

_____

MINDFUL STRENGTH

STRENGTH LOOKS DIFFERENT FOR you every day—some days it looks like surrendering, and others it looks like owning your power. The goal is not to have a single version of strength, but to tap into whatever type of strength you need in any given moment. To do so you need to be mindful and self-aware.

———————————————

Use the following simple practices to cultivate your sense of mindfulness and self-awareness.

- Eat slowly and intentionally. Notice the tastes, textures, and temperature, even saying them to yourself in your head.

- When you move your body, notice the way your body feels, and which muscles assist and allow for the movement.

- Tune in to your breathing when you get into bed at night. Is it fast? Is it slow? Is it labored?

Different areas of your life demand strength in different ways. Write down at least three areas of your life that demand strength and explain what it looks like to be strong in each one. For example, the strength you need as a mother might look different from the strength you need as an employee.

_____

_____

_____

_____

_____

_____

_____

_____

_____

_____

_____

_____

_____

_____

_____

_____

_____

How has your definition of strength evolved since childhood? Write what your definition of strength was at age ten, twenty, thirty, and so on, adding your own definition of strength for each decade that you've been alive. Take time to reflect on how your definition of strength has changed and what caused those changes.

_____

_____

_____

_____

_____

_____

_____

_____

_____

_____

_____

_____

_____

_____

_____

THE FOUR-WEEK CHALLENGE

When you challenge yourself physically, you build mental strength as well. Think about it: To complete a hard physical challenge, you must psych yourself up or tell yourself to push through, even when you don't want to. This builds mental strength and agility.

For this exercise, task yourself with one physical challenge each week for four weeks. Write down each challenge and put a checkmark in the "completed" box once it's finished. Finally, write about how your mental strength improved as a result. What did you learn? What were you forced to face? How can you apply that strength to other areas of your life?

	PHYSICAL CHALLENGE	COMPLETED?	STRENGTH IMPROVEMENTS
WEEK 1			
WEEK 2			
WEEK 3			
WEEK 4			

Sometimes being kind is an act of strength. Think back to a time in your life when it took strength to be kind to someone. Describe the situation and how it felt to be kind in that difficult moment. Finally, reflect on a lesson you learned that can support you now.

_____

_____

_____

_____

_____

_____

_____

_____

_____

_____

_____

_____

_____

_____

_____

_____

_____

Strength isn't just in your mind; you feel it in your body, too. List three different times when you had to be strong and how that strength felt in your body. For example, when speaking up for yourself, you might have had shaky hands but felt your shoulders pull back with confidence.

_____

_____

_____

_____

_____

_____

_____

_____

_____

_____

_____

_____

_____

_____

_____

_____

_____

SUMMON YOUR STRENGTH WITH A MANTRA

IT'S NOT ALWAYS EASY being strong. It often feels easier to walk away or to take the path of least resistance. Luckily, you can tap into that strength with a mantra, which is a phrase that helps anchor you in your strength. If a moment arises when it's hard to find your strength, you can repeat your mantra to feel strong again.

Find a quiet space to sit for five to ten minutes. Take three deep breaths to turn your attention inward and center yourself. Return your breath to normal and recall a moment when you didn't feel strong. Give your past self a pep talk.

During your pep talk, listen for a phrase that stands out to you most—that will become your mantra. For example, you might say, "You are so powerful and strong, you know what to do, nothing can stop you," and the phrase *Nothing can stop you* stands out most to you. That becomes your mantra.

Asking for support is a sign of strength. Instead of trying to do it all, create an "ad" for your life. Make a list of all the tasks you would like help with—and the person or thing that can help you with each one. Now, take action and ask for support on at least one task.

_____

_____

_____

_____

_____

_____

_____

_____

_____

_____

_____

_____

_____

_____

_____

_____

_____

_____

In which areas of your life would you like to show more strength? More importantly, what does being stronger in those areas look like for you? Use this time to write about three areas where you want to have more strength and ideas for how you can cultivate it.

_____

_____

_____

_____

_____

_____

_____

_____

_____

_____

_____

_____

_____

_____

_____

SEE ALL THE COLORS OF YOUR STRENGTH

There are many ways you show your strength every day, and in every area of your life. But they can be hard to recognize and appreciate. It's time to take a step back and see all the colors of your strength.

Look at yourself through the eyes of someone who sees your strength: your best friend, a parent, co-worker, or partner. As you do, write down the times you are or have been strong but didn't give yourself as much credit as you should have. You may be tempted to think, *Oh, no one thinks I'm strong*, but that's *you* talking, not your loved one. Let that voice float away. Instead, sink into the voice of the person who loves you.

I am/was strong when I _____

_____.

I am/was strong when I _____

_____.

I am/was strong when I _____

_____.

I am/was strong when I _____

_____.

You can gain strength by empowering others to be strong. What are some ways you can empower the people around you to be stronger? Consider every area of your life from work (co-workers) to your personal life (children, partner, or best friend) and write what you can do and when you can do it.

_____

_____

_____

_____

_____

_____

_____

_____

_____

_____

_____

_____

_____

_____

_____

What does it mean to you to be physically fit? How can you cultivate that physical strength in a way that feels good for your body? Remember: Physical strength doesn't have to come from lifting weights. Maybe you want to commit to doing yoga two times per week or taking one hike each weekend.

_____

_____

_____

_____

_____

_____

_____

_____

_____

_____

_____

_____

_____

_____

_____

_____

_____

CREATE YOUR STRONG PROFILE

Your strength is unique, like you, and understanding what your version of strength looks like can help you emulate it more often. Create a profile of your strength and tap into how uniquely strong you are, deepening your connection with yourself and your power.

Fill in the blanks below to complete each sentence.

I am strongest when _____.

When I stand firm in my strength, I feel _____.

My proudest moment of strength was _____.

The three words that describe me at my strongest are _____.

I promise to be strong when _____.

I want to become stronger in _____.

I practice my physical strength by _____.

I sharpen my mental strength by _____.

What's the hardest thing you want to achieve or overcome right now? Tap into your ideal world, where you're able to be your strongest self, and answer these questions. In an ideal world, what actions would I take? What would I say? What's the outcome I desire? Writing out the experience now can help you build strength for later.

_____

_____

_____

_____

_____

_____

_____

_____

_____

_____

_____

_____

_____

_____

_____

_____

_____

_____

If you were to describe your strength as a person, how would you describe her? List the characteristics and adjectives that describe who she is, what she looks like, and the strength she radiates. Maybe she walks with her head high, stands firmly connected to the ground, and has bright, piercing eyes.

_____

_____

_____

_____

_____

_____

_____

_____

_____

_____

_____

_____

_____

_____

_____

_____

A LOVE LETTER TO YOURSELF

It can be easy to take your strength for granted because it's just what you do. You know there is no other option, so you do the strong thing when you must. Yet, it's powerful to recognize yourself for that hard work and that's what you'll do today.

Write your strongest self a love letter. You might tell her how proud you are of all that she's done. You might empathize with her, saying that you know how hard it is to be so strong. Don't be afraid to use terms of endearment, like *my love* or *darling*.

    If you're struggling to get started, think of your strongest self as your best friend, partner, or loved one. What would you say to him or her in this letter? Let that kindness and compassion be your guide.

_____

_____

_____

_____

_____

_____

_____

_____

_____

_____

_____

_____

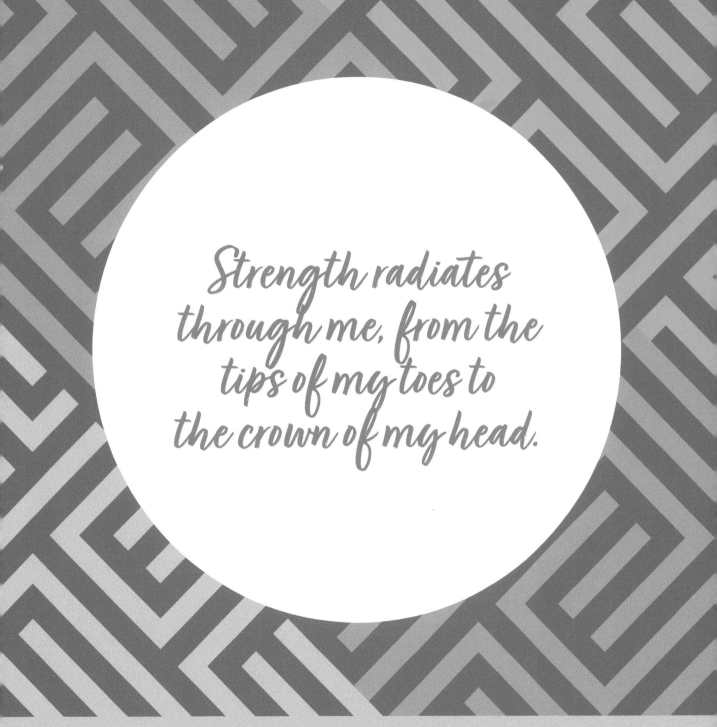

Strength radiates through me, from the tips of my toes to the crown of my head.

DISCOVER WHAT FUELS YOU

IT'S ONE THING TO know the kind of strong woman you want to be. It's another thing to take action and *be* that person. You must be the one to set yourself up for success first and foremost. The best way to do that is to understand what empowers you to be a strong woman.

Conversely, it's important to understand what disempowers you—what makes you feel weak, less than, or incapable. When you know what brings you down, you can avoid or eliminate that and instead focus on what lifts you up.

Get ready to know yourself more deeply and uncover what motivates you to be a strong woman.

I choose to focus on what empowers me and walk away from anything or anyone that doesn't.

Having a support system is critical to feeling empowered and strong. Map out your current support system. Make a list of the people who make you feel strong and pay attention to any gaps. Do you need more support in certain areas of your life?

_____

_____

_____

_____

_____

_____

_____

_____

_____

_____

_____

_____

_____

_____

_____

Continually spending time with people who disempower you slowly erodes your strength. Create a list of people who disempower you and, beside each name, share at least one way for you to distance yourself from them, their words, or their actions.

_____

_____

_____

_____

_____

_____

_____

_____

_____

_____

_____

_____

_____

_____

_____

_____

_____

"I AM" AFFIRMATIONS

AN "I AM" AFFIRMATION is a powerful form of affirmation because it encourages you to affirm that you're already the person you want to be. This type of affirmation is most beneficial when repeated consistently. The more you say it, the deeper you believe it, the easier it is to *be* it.

Choose three to five "I am" affirmations from the following list that feel most relevant to the strong woman you want to be. Repeat them three times each morning before you get out of bed and every night when you get into bed. By stacking the affirmations with something you already do, like getting into bed, it's easier to form a habit.

Use the empty spaces to write your own "I am" affirmations if you have a few in mind.

☐ I am powerful.

☐ I am unstoppable.

☐ I am kind.

☐ I am confident.

☐ I am adaptable.

☐ I am vulnerable.

☐ I am independent.

☐ I am ready for any challenge.

☐ I am capable.

☐ I am tough.

☐ I am strong-willed.

☐ I am bold.

☐ I am _____.

☐ I am _____.

☐ I am _____.

☐ I am _____.

☐ I am _____.

What do you need to change in your life to feel stronger every day?

Consider the routines, habits, situations, and people that keep you from being your strongest self. All these factors play a role in whether you're able to tap into your strength when you need it.

_____

_____

_____

_____

_____

_____

_____

_____

_____

_____

_____

_____

_____

_____

_____

_____

_____

_____

How do you disempower yourself? Do you use negative self-talk, lack self-compassion, or let critical thoughts keep you from feeling and being strong? Be honest and make a list of all the ways you disempower yourself. Also, be gentle with yourself. Use this as a self-awareness tool, not an opportunity to self-criticize.

_____

_____

_____

_____

_____

_____

_____

_____

_____

_____

_____

_____

_____

_____

_____

CREATE YOUR EMPOWERING DAILY ROUTINE

Your daily actions have a significant impact on whether you can empower yourself to be a stronger person. They are a mirror for your life, so it's time to rethink your daily routine and create one that's set up to empower you every day.

Below is a checklist of things you can add to your daily routine. Put a check next to three to five items you plan to incorporate throughout your day. It can be tempting to choose more than that, but if you overestimate what you can do, you risk getting overwhelmed and giving up altogether.

☐ Write in your journal

☐ Meditate

☐ Do yoga

☐ Stretch your body

☐ Lift weights

☐ Do cardio (hiking, running, swimming, etc.)

☐ Set intentions

☐ Plan your day

☐ Drink hot lemon water

☐ Eat nutritious foods

☐ Repeat "I am" affirmations

☐ Set aside time for daily planning

☐ Make your bed

☐ Read

☐ Connect with a loved one

☐ Take a midday break

☐ Unwind at the end of the day

☐ Create (paint, color, ceramics, etc.)

☐ Replace one cup of coffee with tea

☐ Listen to a podcast

☐ Visualize your strength

☐ Spend time reflecting

☐ Clean your space

How can you fill your cup when it feels empty? Consider actions you can do daily, weekly, monthly, and annually to tap back into your strength. Consider things like movement, connection, reflection—but be specific. What kind of movement will you do? What tools will you use to reflect?

_____

_____

_____

_____

_____

_____

_____

_____

_____

_____

_____

_____

_____

_____

_____

Walking away from situations that disempower you can be hard. For example, leaving a disempowering job means you need to find a better one to replace it, but that doesn't happen overnight. However, you can still make the experience more manageable. Use this time to brainstorm three to five shifts you can make to improve current disempowering situations.

_____

_____

_____

_____

_____

_____

_____

_____

_____

_____

_____

_____

_____

_____

_____

_____

_____

CREATE MENTAL SPACE TO EMPOWER YOURSELF

LOVED ONES, FRIENDS, AND partners often have the best intentions when their words or actions make you feel disempowered, but it still hurts. You may not feel strong enough to stand up to them or stand up for yourself. This practice will help you create a strong mental space for yourself before, after, and during your time with these people, so you can come back to your strength when you need it most.

BEFORE: Choose an affirmation that makes you feel strong and empowered, like one from this journal.

DURING: When you begin to feel disempowered, repeat the affirmation in your head followed by this reminder: "What they say or do is a reflection of them, not me."

AFTER: Clear yourself from the disempowering energy by visualizing yourself cutting a cord that runs between you and that person(s) or situation.

The way you start your morning has a significant impact on the rest of your day. Envision your ideal, empowering morning and write down what it looks like. What do you make time for? How can you weave some of those things into your morning each day or a few times each week?

_____

_____

_____

_____

_____

_____

_____

_____

_____

_____

_____

_____

_____

_____

_____

_____

_____

Recall a time when you felt truly empowered. Who were you with? What were you doing? More importantly, how can you replicate that experience? For example, if you left a networking event feeling ready to take on the world, you could plan to go to more of those events.

_____

_____

_____

_____

_____

_____

_____

_____

_____

_____

_____

_____

_____

_____

_____

_____

_____

_____

DISCOVER WHAT DISEMPOWERS YOU

It's not always easy to recognize who or what disempowers you. If you've been experiencing disempowering people and situations for a long time, it begins to feel normal. Use this exercise to shine a light on the disempowering experiences and people you've overlooked. When you know who or what is disempowering you, it becomes more possible for you to take action.

Answer the following questions. Give yourself time to go through each one and, most important, be honest with yourself.

When was the last time you felt disempowered? What happened?

_____

_____

_____

_____

Who makes you feel less than or not strong enough? What do they say or do?

_____

_____

_____

_____

What situation(s) makes you feel disempowered? How often are you in this situation?

_____

_____

_____

_____

_____

_____

How do you react when you are being disempowered? (For example, you might shut down and get quiet or you might push back and get frustrated.)

_____

_____

_____

_____

_____

_____

You learn by watching others who are already doing what you hope to achieve. Who is your greatest role model for empowerment? It can be someone you know personally or someone you just know of. What does she do to empower herself and others, and how can you adopt those same qualities in your life and way of living?

_____

_____

_____

_____

_____

_____

_____

_____

_____

_____

_____

_____

_____

_____

_____

_____

_____

_____

Recalling past achievements is a simple way to remember how it feels to be strong and empowered. What achievements are you most proud of? Don't forget to consider achievements in every era and area of your life, from childhood to adult and from personal to professional.

_____

_____

_____

_____

_____

_____

_____

_____

_____

_____

_____

_____

_____

_____

_____

_____

FROM PHYSICAL FITNESS
TO MENTAL STRENGTH

Physical activity can make you feel empowered, which in turn, fuels your strength. Therefore, moving your body is a great way to feel strong and stay empowered every day. The challenge, however, is committing to doing those things that empower you. That's why you need a plan—and now is the perfect time to make one.

Use the following planner to set up your weekly physical activity. Select at least three days each week to move your body in a way that feels empowering, and challenge yourself to stick with it for at least thirty days. Remember to choose times and activities that work with your schedule so you're more likely to stick with them.

DAY	ACTIVITY	SCHEDULED FOR	DONE? YES/NO
MONDAY			
TUESDAY			
WEDNESDAY			
THURSDAY			
FRIDAY			
SATURDAY			
SUNDAY			

Use stream of consciousness to respond to today's prompt. Read the question and just start writing, no questioning or thinking deeply. What is possible for you if you spend more time with people who empower you to be strong? Answer in any format, from writing lists to full sentences.

_____

_____

_____

_____

_____

_____

_____

_____

_____

_____

_____

_____

_____

_____

_____

_____

Motivating yourself to be strong is sometimes the only option, and that's okay. Tap into that self-motivation by thinking about what your most empowered self would say to your disempowered self to lift her up and encourage her to be strong. Write it out as a conversation or letter.

_____

_____

_____

_____

_____

_____

_____

_____

_____

_____

_____

_____

_____

_____

_____

_____

_____

_____

CREATE AN EMPOWERING TO-BE LIST

A to-be list can fuel you to be strong when finding your strength feels next to impossible. On it, you include all the qualities of strength that you want to have. In moments when you need to tap into your strength, return to this list to remember the strong person you want to be.

Create your to-be list right now. Come back to this list regularly to remind yourself of the strong qualities you want to have. You can use this list for as long as you want or create a new one each week based on the challenges you encounter.

- _____
- _____
- _____
- _____
- _____
- _____
- _____
- _____
- _____
- _____
- _____
- _____
- _____

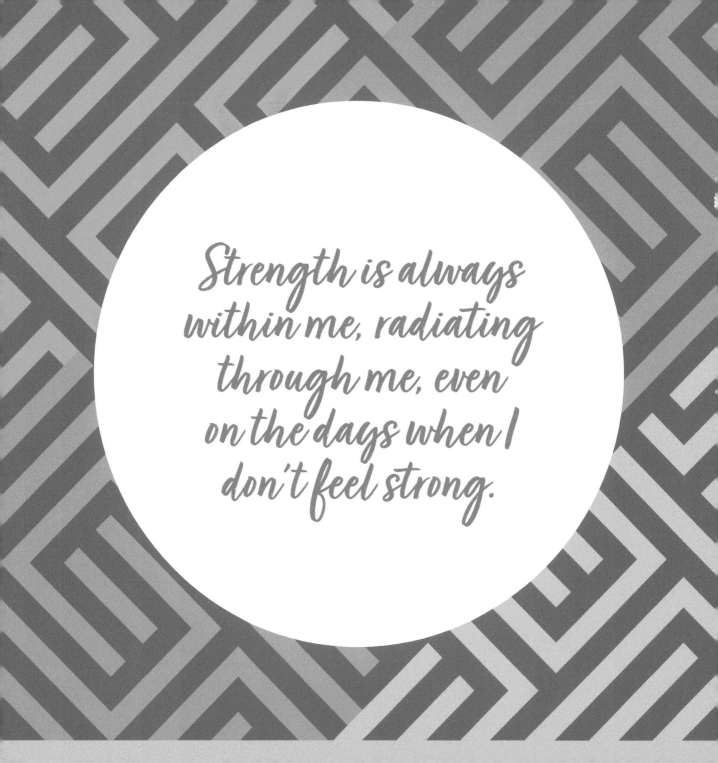

Strength is always within me, radiating through me, even on the days when I don't feel strong.

RECOGNIZE VULNERABILITY AS A STRENGTH

YOUR VULNERABILITY IS NOT a weakness—it's a strength. Allowing yourself to feel vulnerable can be challenging because it requires you to look at things and experience feelings that might make you feel scared, sad, or uncertain. That, however, is exactly why it takes strength to be vulnerable rather than push those feelings away.

This section provides a space for you to be vulnerable, process anything that already makes you feel vulnerable, and see how that vulnerability ultimately makes you stronger. Using tools like self-compassion and self-awareness, you can rethink what vulnerability means and create a better relationship with it.

Allow yourself to be open and honest and, most importantly, sink into the feelings that rise to the surface.

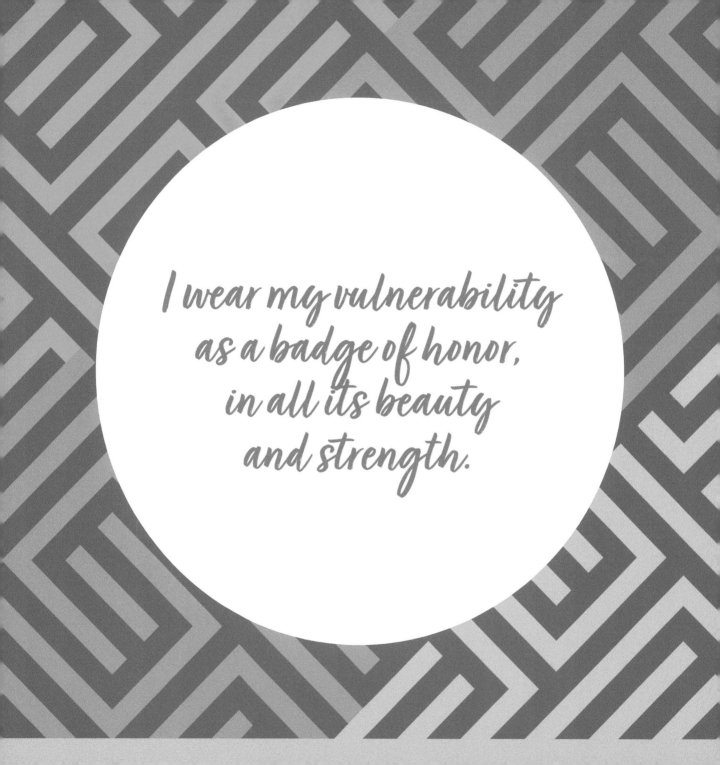

I wear my vulnerability as a badge of honor, in all its beauty and strength.

What makes you feel vulnerable and how do you react? List three to five specific people, places, or experiences that make you feel the most vulnerable, and pair each one with your reaction. Accepting and embracing vulnerability starts with this challenging but important awareness.

_____

_____

_____

_____

_____

_____

_____

_____

_____

_____

_____

_____

_____

_____

_____

_____

_____

What does vulnerability mean to you? How do you know when you're feeling vulnerable? Develop your own profile for vulnerability. When you can spot yourself in a vulnerable state, you can shift your mindset from "this is bad" to "this is making me stronger."

_____

_____

_____

_____

_____

_____

_____

_____

_____

_____

_____

_____

_____

_____

_____

_____

FIND STRENGTH IN YOUR SELF-TALK

IT'S EASY TO BE critical of yourself in moments of weakness. Thoughts like *I'm not good enough* might be flashing through your mind as you beat yourself up. Although those thoughts happen automatically, after many years of self-criticism in vulnerable moments, you can shift them to be positive instead.

Every time you say something critical to yourself, or you feel the urge to do so, counter it with one positive statement. For example, if you struggled through a presentation at work, you might have the urge to say: *Wow, I sucked at that, I'm the worst at giving presentations. I'm so stupid.*

But instead, as you feel that thought arise, intentionally choose one that's filled with self-love. Here are some examples:

Wow, that was hard, good for me for doing that!

I'm proud of myself for doing the best I could.

That was tough, but I learned a lot for next time.

I am my own worst critic; I bet it was much better than I thought.

Sometimes softening, rather than fighting, is the strong thing to do. In what areas of your life can softening your response or mindset allow you to be stronger? If this doesn't feel relevant now, recall a time when softening would have made you stronger and how that might apply to your life in the future.

_____

_____

_____

_____

_____

_____

_____

_____

_____

_____

_____

_____

_____

_____

_____

_____

Self-compassion is a sign of strength. It shows that you know your power, value, and worth. List five ways you can show self-compassion this week. Choose one of the ideas to repeat every day, building it into your daily routine to develop deeper compassion for yourself.

_____

_____

_____

_____

_____

_____

_____

_____

_____

_____

_____

_____

_____

_____

_____

_____

REWRITE THE STORY

Although you can't change what happened in the past, you can reflect on a difficult situation and see the strength you had in that moment, not just your vulnerability. Looking back like this is a powerful way to change the way you think about your vulnerability in the future.

Example: *I felt vulnerable when I told my best friend that her words hurt me. This was a strong moment because I was standing up for myself, which isn't always easy to do, especially with a close friend.*

_____

I felt vulnerable when . . .

_____

_____

_____

_____

This was a strong moment because . . .

_____

_____

_____

_____

It's easier to see vulnerability as a strength in others than it is to see it in yourself. Think back to a time when someone you love was vulnerable. Describe the person's strength at that moment. You can write a list or use a story-telling format.

_____

_____

_____

_____

_____

_____

_____

_____

_____

_____

_____

_____

_____

_____

_____

_____

Reflect on the last time you felt vulnerable and become your own hype girl. If you were standing outside yourself, how would you have supported and hyped yourself at that moment? What would you have said or told yourself to do?

_____

_____

_____

_____

_____

_____

_____

_____

_____

_____

_____

_____

_____

_____

_____

_____

NORMALIZE YOUR VULNERABILITY

WHEN YOU FEEL ALONE in your vulnerability, it can lead to more self-criticism and frustration. When you normalize the feeling, you remember that there's nothing wrong with you.

Instead of letting yourself get lost in the sense of isolation, normalize it for yourself.
   For example, if you're struggling to stick with your workout routine, you can normalize that vulnerability by saying to yourself,

> *So many people struggle to create and stick with a workout routine. Life is hectic and things come up. That makes it challenging to maintain a consistent program. I even know some friends who have struggled with this same thing. I'm not alone. I'll find a schedule that works for my life.*

The more often you can shift vulnerability and remember you're not alone, the easier it is to tap into your strength to turn it around.

What parts of yourself do you need to embrace to see the strength in your vulnerability? Perhaps you need to embrace your emotional side, the part of you that wants to feel the full rainbow of emotions. List all the parts of you that show up when you're feeling vulnerable and why you're grateful for each one.

_____

_____

_____

_____

_____

_____

_____

_____

_____

_____

_____

_____

_____

_____

_____

_____

_____

_____

How do you react to vulnerability in others? If you judge or criticize, write down how you can practice being more supportive to them. If you're empathetic, journal about how you can be more empathetic to yourself as well.

_____

_____

_____

_____

_____

_____

_____

_____

_____

_____

_____

_____

_____

_____

_____

_____

TEN DAYS OF VULNERABILITY

Intentionally putting yourself in vulnerable situations or taking vulnerable actions can help you see why being vulnerable is a test of your strength, rather than a moment of weakness. It can also remind you that feeling vulnerable is a normal part of life—not something to be ashamed of.

Practice being vulnerable for the next ten days with these challenges.

1. Do something you're not good at.

2. Try something you're scared of.

3. Talk to a stranger.

4. Tell someone you're upset with them.

5. Share a personal story with a close friend.

6. Ask for help.

7. Tell someone you're grateful for them (and why).

8. Apologize to someone.

9. Tell someone else why you're proud of yourself.

10. Introduce yourself to someone new.

Write about your reactions and responses to the concept of vulnerability. What does it bring up for you? Memories of past experiences? Intense emotions?

_____

_____

_____

_____

_____

_____

_____

_____

_____

_____

_____

_____

_____

_____

_____

_____

Forgiveness is an act of courage, and it takes a lot of vulnerability. Write yourself a letter of forgiveness and do the same for someone else you want to forgive. Simply writing it down or typing it out can help relieve the frustration or anger while allowing you to practice being vulnerable in a safe space.

_____

_____

_____

_____

_____

_____

_____

_____

_____

_____

_____

_____

_____

_____

_____

_____

_____

YOUR VULNERABILITY PERMISSION SLIP

Giving yourself permission to be vulnerable can feel like taking back your power. Instead of being at the whim of vulnerability, you choose it—you embrace it. So go ahead, give yourself a permission slip to be vulnerable.

Fill in the blanks below and use your permission slip every time you need to be vulnerable.

I, _____ (YOUR NAME),

GIVE MYSELF PERMISSION TO FEEL VULNERABLE.

IT'S OKAY IF I FEEL _____ BECAUSE THAT'S

NORMAL AND SHOWS THAT I AM _____.

WHEN I ALLOW MYSELF TO BE VULNERABLE, I ALSO MODEL IT

FOR _____ , AND MY VULNERABILITY

GIVES OTHERS THE COURAGE TO BE VULNERABLE, TOO.

SIGNATURE _____ DATE _____.

Surrendering is an act of vulnerability. It can be challenging to do because it feels as if you're quitting, giving up, or losing your power. Shift back into your strength by remembering what you *don't* have to give up when you surrender. Finish the following sentence:

Surrendering doesn't mean I have to . . .

_____

_____

_____

_____

_____

_____

_____

_____

_____

_____

_____

_____

_____

_____

_____

_____

You don't need to apologize to yourself or others for being vulnerable. Instead, you can stand in your power and be unapologetic for choosing and doing what's right for you. Make a list of vulnerable moments that you won't apologize for. Embrace those moments, and the strength you're showing, by claiming them.

_____

_____

_____

_____

_____

_____

_____

_____

_____

_____

_____

_____

_____

_____

_____

_____

NAME THE FEELINGS

What other feelings come up when you experience vulnerability? Shame? Fear? Embarrassment? Understanding and naming the less-comfortable feelings is a powerful way to bring awareness to what's happening inside and remind yourself that these feelings are normal and okay. Instead of getting lost in the moment, you can bring awareness to what you're feeling, practice self-compassion, and make a shift.

Practice this by thinking back to the last time you felt vulnerable. Which feelings from the word bank best describe how you were feeling? Circle the ones that resonate most. Next time you're feeling vulnerable, mentally "circle" the feelings that are coming up so you can acknowledge them and then shift.

Depleted	Frustrated	Self-conscious
Helpless	Grouchy	Worthless
Sensitive	Impatient	Frazzled
Hopeless	Irritated	Restless
Agitated	Resentful	Worn out
Cynical	Lonely	Cynical
Edgy	Hesitant	

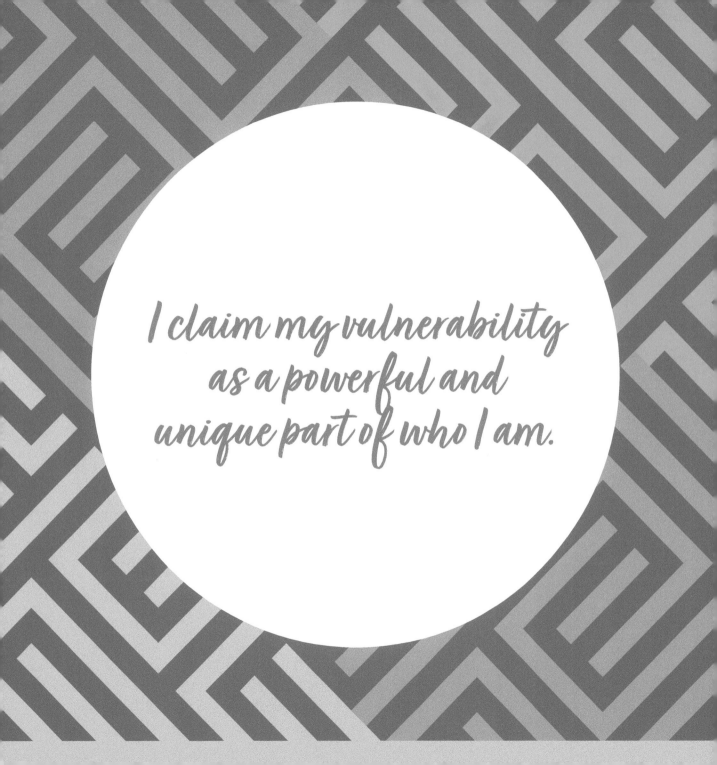

I claim my vulnerability as a powerful and unique part of who I am.

BUILD YOUR CONFIDENCE

YOU KNOW A CONFIDENT woman when you see one. It's the way she carries herself and the way she talks. You can feel the confidence and it is contagious. You may have even thought to yourself, *I wish I could be that confident*.

The good news is, you can. Even more importantly, you *must,* because that confidence powers your strength. If you need to walk away from someone, being confident in your choice gives you the strength to take those steps. If you need to speak up for yourself, being confident in your worth allows you to keep going even when your voice is shaking.

If you feel like you need a confidence boost, this section was made for you. It's time to cultivate your confidence with intention.

Confidence is always available to me; all I must do is choose it.

Rate your confidence on a scale of 1 to 10, with 1 being the least confident and 10 being the most confident. Explain why you gave yourself this rating and how this rating has changed over the years. Were you more confident five years ago? Why?

_____

_____

_____

_____

_____

_____

_____

_____

_____

_____

_____

_____

_____

_____

_____

_____

Sometimes confidence comes naturally—you don't have to think about it. In which situations do you feel natural confidence? What are you doing? Who are you talking to? Why do you feel so confident?

_____

_____

_____

_____

_____

_____

_____

_____

_____

_____

_____

_____

_____

_____

_____

_____

THE CONFIDENCE CHALLENGE

ONE WAY TO BUILD your confidence is to put yourself in situations where you struggle to be confident. It's easy to stay in your comfort zone and avoid things that don't come as naturally or are difficult for you. However, practice makes perfect—and confidence is something you can practice with intention.

Choose three scenarios where you lack confidence and put yourself in each scenario at least once this week. This can be as simple as reaching out to a friend or acquaintance you'd like to get to know better or attending a networking event if you usually avoid them. Write down your three scenarios and check the box when you finish each one.

☐ _____

_____

_____

☐ _____

_____

_____

☐ _____

_____

_____

Recall a time when you were trying to be confident. How did you find inspiration to feel strong, even when you were scared?

_____

_____

_____

_____

_____

_____

_____

_____

_____

_____

_____

_____

_____

_____

_____

_____

_____

_____

Revisit a specific time when you felt completely confident. What were you doing? Why were you so confident? How did it feel to have that confidence? If possible, seek out this experience, or one similar, more often, allowing yourself to tap into your confidence again and again.

_____

_____

_____

_____

_____

_____

_____

_____

_____

_____

_____

_____

_____

_____

_____

_____

THE RIPPLE EFFECT OF CONFIDENCE

The amazing thing about confidence is that it's so much more than just confidence. When you feel confident, you're also powerful and self-assured. This makes practicing your confidence a powerful tool for building strength.

Get to know who you are in your most confident moments. Check the qualities that complete this sentence for you: When I am confident, I am also . . .

☐ Powerful   ☐ Determined

☐ Courageous   ☐ Tenacious

☐ Proud   ☐ Certain

☐ Beautiful   ☐ Influential

☐ Fulfilled   ☐ Energetic

☐ Assured   ☐ Hopeful

Whose confidence inspires you the most? List their characteristics and give at least one example of when you experienced their confidence firsthand. This can be anyone, including someone famous or someone who's no longer alive.

_____

_____

_____

_____

_____

_____

_____

_____

_____

_____

_____

_____

_____

_____

_____

_____

_____

_____

It's time to give yourself a confidence boost. What are you really good at? Make the list as long as you can from your personal and professional life. Are you a great friend? Are you always punctual? Are you the most efficient person at your job?

_____

_____

_____

_____

_____

_____

_____

_____

_____

_____

_____

_____

_____

_____

_____

THE ENERGY OF CONFIDENCE VISUALIZATION

YOU NOTICE THE ENERGY of a confident person often before they even speak. Tap into and cultivate the energy of confidence with this simple visualization exercise.

1. Find a comfortable place to sit or lie down and close your eyes.

2. Take three deep breaths in and out, centering yourself and turning your mind inward.

3. Return to your regular breathing and visualize a bright yellow light above your head. That's the energy of confidence.

4. Visualize the crown of your head opening and allowing that light to enter.

5. See the energy of confidence flowing through your body, into every cell. You are filled with this light and it's now surrounding your body in a cocoon of bright yellow, confident energy.

6. Once you've sunk into this energy and let it fill every inch of you, come back to the space you're in.

7. Take three deep breaths to finish the practice and open your eyes.

Use this visualization whenever you want to tap into your strongest, most confident self.

What negative words do you associate with confidence? Replace those words with new ones to remind yourself that being confident isn't a bad thing. For example, you might replace "arrogant" with "self-assured," remembering that being self-assured is far from a negative attribute.

_____

_____

_____

_____

_____

_____

_____

_____

_____

_____

_____

_____

_____

_____

_____

_____

_____

See the connection between confidence and strength in your life. Recall at least three times in your life when you were strong and how confident you felt. Although it may not be obvious on the surface, even a small amount of confidence is all you need sometimes.

_____

_____

_____

_____

_____

_____

_____

_____

_____

_____

_____

_____

_____

_____

_____

UNDERSTANDING YOUR CONFIDENCE

When do you feel most confident? When does it feel a little shaky? Knowing this can help you appreciate your confidence and identify the times when you need to develop more of it.

Finish the following sentences. There may be more than one response you want to include for each one, so allow yourself to be thorough.

I am confident in my ability to _____

_____.

I feel most confident when I _____

_____.

My confidence is shaky when I _____

_____.

I want to be more confident when _____

_____.

The most confident role I've ever played in my life is _____

_____.

The last time I felt confident was _____

_____.

Give yourself five compliments right now—big and small. Write each one down, and as you do, say it out loud to yourself. Choose one that you'll repeat to yourself at least three more times throughout the day. Bonus points for choosing one to repeat to yourself for the rest of the week.

_____

_____

_____

_____

_____

_____

_____

_____

_____

_____

_____

_____

_____

_____

_____

_____

_____

Sometimes confidence works from the outside in. If you feel good about how you look, you'll be more confident in your actions. What outfit (that you already own) makes you feel most confident in yourself? Describe the entire look, from your hair to your shoes, and plan at least one day this week to wear that exact outfit.

_____

_____

_____

_____

_____

_____

_____

_____

_____

_____

_____

_____

_____

_____

_____

_____

_____

I CHOOSE CONFIDENCE

Self-doubt, fear, and similar feelings can easily take the place of strength when confidence is lacking. Although the feelings may be valid and real, you don't have to let them run the show. You can choose to replace them with strength and confidence.

Use this exercise to release the feelings that are taking space away from your strength and confidence. Go beyond self-doubt to include other feelings that hold you back, such as fear or worry.

I choose confidence instead of _____.

I choose confidence instead of _____.

I choose confidence instead of _____.

I choose confidence instead of _____.

I choose confidence instead of _____.

I choose confidence instead of _____.

I choose confidence instead of _____.

Write your confidence a thank-you letter. Thank it for being there when you needed it and for helping you summon your strength. Speak kindly to this part of yourself and be specific, listing moments when you were most thankful for its presence.

_____

_____

_____

_____

_____

_____

_____

_____

_____

_____

_____

_____

_____

_____

_____

_____

_____

After completing each exercise, journal prompt, and practice in this section, re-rate your confidence on a scale of 1 to 10, with 1 being the least confident and 10 being the most confident. Explain why you gave yourself this rating and how you feel now versus when you started the section.

_____

_____

_____

_____

_____

_____

_____

_____

_____

_____

_____

_____

_____

_____

_____

SHARE YOUR CONFIDENCE

Don't keep your confidence to yourself. Once you have it, you can share it with others so they can feel confident, too. You can be that person that people look at and say, Wow, I wish I was that confident.

Use this exercise to choose a few people you're going to share your confidence with this week. The fun thing about this exercise is how great it feels to make someone else feel good. Make it a regular habit to help others see their own confidence while gaining more confidence in yourself.

I will send an encouraging email or text message to _____

_____.

I will celebrate _____ for _____

_____.

I will encourage _____ to _____

_____.

I will remind _____ how brilliant she is.

I will empower _____ to finally _____.

My confidence grows stronger with each passing day.

NURTURE YOUR WHOLE SELF

TO BE STRONG, YOU must take care of yourself. If you're always surviving and never thriving, it can be hard to dig deep for your strength when you need it most. That's why it's important to prioritize self-care, celebration, and moments of nurturing as often as possible.

I know what you're thinking: *I don't have time for that!* What you'll learn in this section is that you don't need to carve out hours of time to nurture yourself. Even just five minutes each day can make a difference in how you feel now and in the long term.

Use this section to discover how easy it can be to nurture yourself with simple habits and routines. You may be surprised at how good you feel when you surrender to taking care of yourself.

I show up for myself before I show up for the rest of the world.

You may not nurture yourself because you're stuck in old beliefs that say you're not worthy or good enough. Reflect on at least three beliefs that are holding you back from nurturing yourself. What are they? Where do they come from? Why aren't they true?

_____

_____

_____

_____

_____

_____

_____

_____

_____

_____

_____

_____

_____

_____

_____

_____

_____

How can you nurture yourself every single morning? Even if you have only five minutes before getting out of bed or ten minutes in the car while heading to an appointment, what are a few simple things you can do during the available time that will make you feel good?

_____

_____

_____

_____

_____

_____

_____

_____

_____

_____

_____

_____

_____

_____

_____

_____

_____

THREE THINGS I LOVE ABOUT MYSELF ARE . . .

YOUR INNER DIALOGUE PLAYS an important role in your strength. If you're constantly criticizing yourself, do you ever take a moment to recognize your power? Probably not. This self-love practice will help you shift that negative self-talk so you can step into your strength.

———————————

Every time you look in the mirror, say three things you love about yourself. The compliments shouldn't all be physical. Think about every aspect of your identity and all that you do. Here are some examples:

I love that I worked so hard on that presentation and totally nailed it!

I love that I'm such a good friend.

I love how well I take care of my body.

Time can get in the way of doing the nurturing activities we love most, such as enjoying a day at the spa or taking a trip. What are your favorite ways to nurture yourself but that you don't prioritize? How can you enjoy one of those things each month? Even better: Put one of them on the calendar now.

_____

_____

_____

_____

_____

_____

_____

_____

_____

_____

_____

_____

_____

_____

_____

_____

_____

_____

What simple nurturing activities could you realistically do every day but find excuses not to? Think: eating a healthier breakfast or stretching at the end of the day. Write at least ten simple, self-nurturing activities you can weave into your week that you'd normally make an excuse for. Choose one to do each day for the next seven days.

_____

_____

_____

_____

_____

_____

_____

_____

_____

_____

_____

_____

_____

_____

_____

_____

_____

THE DAILY CELEBRATION

Celebrating yourself is an act of self-nurturing because it feels good to say, "Oh yes, I did that!" Instead of waiting for someone else to celebrate you, make a habit of celebrating yourself daily, starting with this exercise.

Find a reason to celebrate yourself every day this week. Each day, write what you're celebrating and reflect on it at the end of the week. Are you surprised? Does this help you see how strong and successful you are?

MONDAY

_____

TUESDAY

_____

WEDNESDAY

_____

THURSDAY

_____

FRIDAY

_____

SATURDAY

_____

SUNDAY

_____

Forgiveness is a powerful form of nurturing. Instead of criticizing and critiquing yourself for mistakes you've made, forgive yourself. Write at least three things you forgive yourself for and say each one out loud using this format:

I forgive myself for _____

_____

_____

_____

_____

_____

_____

_____

_____

_____

_____

_____

_____

_____

_____

_____

_____

Responsibilities can get in the way of nurturing, but often there is a tendency to take on more than necessary rather than asking for help. Make a list of things you can solicit help for, rather than doing them yourself, so you can carve out a little more time to nurture yourself.

_____

_____

_____

_____

_____

_____

_____

_____

_____

_____

_____

_____

_____

_____

_____

_____

_____

SEEK NURTURING MOMENTS

YOU CAN NURTURE YOURSELF every day. Little things, even if you do them for five minutes, can make a huge difference.

———————————

Use this list to come up with some ideas and then nurture yourself a bit every day for at least one week. Notice how much stronger you can be when you feel rejuvenated from these little moments of self-care.

- Take a bath
- Meditate
- Read a book
- Watch a favorite movie
- Stay in your pajamas
- Binge your favorite show
- Take a walk
- Work out
- Stretch
- Have an extra cup of tea
- Stay in bed a little longer

- Catch up with someone you love
- Drink more water
- Do your nails
- Write in your journal
- Get dressed up for no reason
- Order in your favorite meal
- _____
- _____
- _____
- _____

Appreciating yourself nurtures your soul. Start a gratitude list for the body parts that you take for granted and include why you're grateful for that body part. For example, you might write, *I am grateful for my legs because they allow me to walk to my favorite ice cream shop.*

_____

_____

_____

_____

_____

_____

_____

_____

_____

_____

_____

_____

_____

_____

_____

_____

_____

_____

Saying no is an act of nurturing because if you say yes when you don't mean it, you put others' needs ahead of your own. When have you recently said yes when you didn't want to? Why did you say yes and how can you avoid doing that again in the future?

_____

_____

_____

_____

_____

_____

_____

_____

_____

_____

_____

_____

_____

_____

_____

_____

_____

THE COMMITMENT CONTRACT

You've committed to so many people and things—but have you ever truly committed to yourself? When you're not so depleted because you've taken time to fill up, it's easier to tap into your own strength.

It's time to truly commit to yourself. Fill in the blanks, then sign and date the contract. Let this empower you to commit to your own needs once and for all.

I, _____ (YOUR NAME),

AM COMMITTING TO MYSELF.

IN GIVING MYSELF LOVE AND ATTENTION, I AM ALSO MAKING IT

EASIER TO TAP INTO MY OWN STRENGTH WHENEVER I NEED IT.

I COMMIT TO THESE THREE WEEKLY ACTS OF SELF-NURTURING:

_____

_____

_____

BY MAKING THIS COMMITMENT, I PROMISE TO CARE MORE DEEPLY

FOR MYSELF.

SIGNATURE: _____ DATE: _____

How often do you take time to nurture your imagination? Use this time to imagine your ideal life. What are you doing? Who are you with? Where are you? Have fun with this—there are no limits to your imagination!

_____

_____

_____

_____

_____

_____

_____

_____

_____

_____

_____

_____

_____

_____

_____

_____

_____

_____

_____

Spending more time taking care of yourself can have incredible benefits, from feeling stronger to being a kinder partner. How can nurturing yourself improve your life? Be specific. What areas of your life would change? How might your mood or energy improve? How might your relationships evolve?

_____

_____

_____

_____

_____

_____

_____

_____

_____

_____

_____

_____

_____

_____

_____

_____

PRACTICE MINDFUL MOVEMENT

Time outside has been proven to reduce stress and improve health. This makes it a powerful act of self-nurturing. Nurture your mind, body, and health by practicing mindful movement outside this week.

While outside, be aware of everything you're experiencing, starting with physical sensations. Notice the points of contact between your body and the earth, how the air feels, or how your body sways front to back. During this movement, take a moment to stop and tap into all your available senses. As you do, fill in the blanks:

I'm sensing _____

_____.

I'm sensing _____

_____.

I'm sensing _____

_____.

I'm sensing _____

_____.

I'm sensing _____

_____.

What preconceived notions about self-care and nurturing do you need to release? Do you think it's too indulgent? Do you think it would take too much time? Put these assumptions on paper so you can begin to overcome them rather than succumb to them.

_____

_____

_____

_____

_____

_____

_____

_____

_____

_____

_____

_____

_____

_____

_____

_____

_____

_____

How can you see your daily responsibilities as nurturing rather than as a burden or something you need to "get through?" For example, packing yourself a lunch is as much an act of love as it was when your parents did it for you as a kid. Write a list of your daily responsibilities and how they nurture you.

_____

_____

_____

_____

_____

_____

_____

_____

_____

_____

_____

_____

_____

_____

_____

_____

SET TECHNOLOGY BOUNDARIES

You're surrounded by technology every day, but you don't have to let yourself get lost in it. By staying constantly "connected" you're also disconnecting from yourself—including your strength and power.

The goal of this exercise is to create guidelines that allow you to disconnect daily and, in turn, reconnect with yourself. Choose at least two boundaries to follow, write your own, or do a combination of both.

- No cell phones or laptops in bed.

- No emails until after having morning coffee or tea.

- Power down your laptop before sitting down for dinner.

- Limited or no use of social media on Sundays.

- Put your phone on silent from 7:00 p.m. to 7:00 a.m.

- Charge your cell phone in another room overnight.

- No cell phones at the dinner table.

- _____

- _____

- _____

With each act of self-nurturing, my strength grows.

SET GOALS THAT MOTIVATE YOU

TO BECOME A STRONGER woman, you must set challenging goals that push you out of your comfort zone. With each goal you set and achieve, you become stronger, more confident, and assured in your strength.

These goals should be both internal, who you want to be, and external, what you want to achieve. As you've learned in this journal, being stronger is as mental and emotional as it is physical, and your goals should reflect that.

However, not all goals are created equal. Simply deciding you want to do something isn't going to help you become a stronger woman. In this section, you'll set clear and powerful goals that make you stronger, while reflecting on why you haven't achieved certain goals in the past and celebrating the many that you have.

With each goal I set, I become stronger; with each goal I achieve, I become unstoppable.

Recall a time when you set a goal and achieved it. How did you get there? What risks did you take? What sacrifices did you make? Remind yourself how you achieved an important goal so you can repeat that again.

_____

_____

_____

_____

_____

_____

_____

_____

_____

_____

_____

_____

_____

_____

_____

_____

_____

What mental blocks get in the way of achieving your goals? We are often the one stopping ourselves from achieving what we want. Get clear on your mental blocks now so you can watch out for them later.

_____

_____

_____

_____

_____

_____

_____

_____

_____

_____

_____

_____

_____

_____

_____

_____

_____

_____

VISUALIZE WHAT YOU DESIRE

BEFORE YOU CAN SET any goals, you must know who you want to be or what you want to achieve. This work needs to be done from the heart, not the head. When you set goals from your head, limitations quickly get in the way.

Use this practice to tap into what you truly desire so you can set goals to get there. Find a quiet space to sit or lie down and take three deep breaths, centering yourself and turning inward. Return to your normal breathing and release all "logic" around what you think you can become or achieve.

Instead, tune in to what your ideal world looks like. What do you want to accomplish? Who do you want to be? Let your imagination run wild; it's here that you'll tap into what you truly want—not what you think you *should* want.

Everyone has excuses, but whether you let them win is what dictates your success. Write at least five excuses you've given when trying to achieve a certain goal. See these excuses for what they are: obstacles standing in your way of becoming stronger and more successful.

_____

_____

_____

_____

_____

_____

_____

_____

_____

_____

_____

_____

_____

_____

_____

_____

_____

What positive beliefs do you have about yourself that inspire and motivate you to achieve your goals and become a stronger woman? For example, you might believe that you are powerful when you focus on what you want, which fuels you as you work toward your goals.

_____

_____

_____

_____

_____

_____

_____

_____

_____

_____

_____

_____

_____

_____

_____

_____

SET YOUR GOALS AND A TIMELINE

Take yourself back to the visualization practice (page 115). What did you realize you truly want to achieve or become? With that in mind, it's time to create powerful goals that will push your limits and make you stronger in the process.

Write your top three goals—one short-term, one medium-term, and one long-term*—along with when you want to accomplish each one. Remember to consider both internal and external goals and be specific. For example, don't just set a goal to get healthy, set a goal to run a 5K or lose X number of pounds.

Goal #1: _____
_____.

Accomplished by: _____
_____.

Goal #2: _____
_____.

Accomplished by: _____
_____.

Goal #3: _____
_____.

Accomplished by: _____
_____.

* Short term: six months to one year Medium term: one to two years Long-term: three to five years

What's your "why" for each goal that you set? For example, a mother's "why" for getting healthy might be to stay active for her young kids. It's important to know your "why," because when the journey gets tough, you can remind yourself why you're working so hard. Instead of throwing in the towel, you can re-inspire yourself to keep going.

_____

_____

_____

_____

_____

_____

_____

_____

_____

_____

_____

_____

_____

_____

Give yourself a pep talk about how powerful you are. If it helps, pretend that you're talking to your best friend. Be inspiring, motivational, and clear that you believe in her abilities. Once it's written, read the letter out loud to yourself, letting each word land within your heart.

_____

_____

_____

_____

_____

_____

_____

_____

_____

_____

_____

_____

_____

_____

_____

_____

_____

FEEL THE ENERGY OF SUCCESS

YOU'VE BEEN SUCCESSFUL MANY times in your life. In the moments that you accomplished a goal, you felt the energy of success. You are an energetic being, and energy attracts like energy. Therefore, it's powerful to continually tap back into that energy, allowing yourself to attract more of it.

Recall a time when you were successful. What were you wearing? What were you doing? What did you achieve? Be in the moment once again. Tune in to how it feels to be successful. Maybe your heart is pounding, or your stomach is fluttering. Perhaps you feel your chest expand or adrenaline pumping through your veins.

Sink into that feeling. Memorize it swirling through you. This is your energy of success. Tap into this energy regularly to remind yourself how it feels to win, and to attract more of that success your way.

Succeeding can be scary. Once you've achieved a goal, you may wonder, *What's next? How can I ever do better than that? What will people say about it?* List at least three fears you have about succeeding.

_____

_____

_____

_____

_____

_____

_____

_____

_____

_____

_____

_____

_____

_____

_____

_____

_____

_____

The beauty in accomplishing goals is what you get to experience on the other side. Relish the vision of what's possible when you achieve one of your three goals. How will you feel? What will your life look like? How will you and your relationships be different?

_____

_____

_____

_____

_____

_____

_____

_____

_____

_____

_____

_____

_____

_____

_____

CREATE YOUR PLAN

You know your goals and when you want to accomplish them, but now it's time to break them down. The key to successful goal setting is to focus on the little things you need to do to get there. Looking at the big picture can be daunting, but thinking about the next small step can feel more manageable.

Use the chart to write your top three goals and three steps you need to take to achieve each one. For example, if one goal is to save $5,000, one step would be to decide how much you need to put away each week or month to get there.

GOAL	STEP 1	STEP 2	STEP 3

Achieving your goals doesn't help just you. It also helps others because you become a role model for following your dreams and pushing beyond your limits. Who in your life will benefit from you achieving the goals that you've set for yourself and how?

_____

_____

_____

_____

_____

_____

_____

_____

_____

_____

_____

_____

_____

_____

List your top five greatest achievements in life. For each one, write about how it made you stronger, more empowered, and more confident in what you can do. Past successes can be the fuel you need to power yourself forward with current challenges.

_____

_____

_____

_____

_____

_____

_____

_____

_____

_____

_____

_____

_____

_____

_____

_____

_____

PREPARE FOR ANY OBSTACLES

It doesn't matter how much you want to achieve your goals; obstacles will present themselves. It's how you manage the obstacles that determines whether you achieve your goals. The best way to overcome them is to prepare for them.

Use the space to write about three potential obstacles that could get in your way and how you can overcome them. For example, if you want to start your own business while working a full-time job, long hours might be an obstacle because you're exhausted during the week. How will you overcome that? Set aside at least one hour every Sunday morning to work on your business.

OBSTACLE	I WILL OVERCOME THIS BY . . .

Finish this sentence: "I can accomplish anything I set my mind to because . . ." Think of qualities that make you powerful, resources that are available to you, skills that you've acquired. There's so much in your toolbox—remind yourself just how capable you are.

_____

_____

_____

_____

_____

_____

_____

_____

_____

_____

_____

_____

_____

_____

_____

How do you want to be remembered? Write about the legacy you want to leave behind in life and what you hope people will say about you for decades to come.

_____

_____

_____

_____

_____

_____

_____

_____

_____

_____

_____

_____

_____

_____

_____

_____

_____

BECOME SOMEONE WHO
ACHIEVES BIG THINGS

You're already someone who can achieve big things—but you may not see all those qualities within yourself. For example, you're already courageous, but perhaps that courage is buried beneath low self-esteem. The good news is, you can choose to access the qualities of a successful person, but first, you have to identify them.

What qualities do you need to achieve the goals you've set for yourself? List at least five qualities, including how you can embody each one. For example, for courage, you might say, "I can stand up for myself at work more often."

Quality: _____

How you will embody it: _____

Quality: _____

How you will embody it: _____

Quality: _____

How you will embody it: _____

Quality: _____

How you will embody it: _____

Quality: _____

How you will embody it: _____

EMPOWER OTHERS BY EXAMPLE

BECOMING A STRONGER WOMAN isn't just about you—it's about everyone else around you, too. Not only do you model your mindset and behavior to the people in your life, but also your strength and confidence empower others to follow in your footsteps.

In this journal you've focused on how you can become stronger, and now it's time to think about how you can use that strength to empower others, especially other women, and how that can empower you in return.

Use this section to understand how you can support the people around you and become a stronger person in the process.

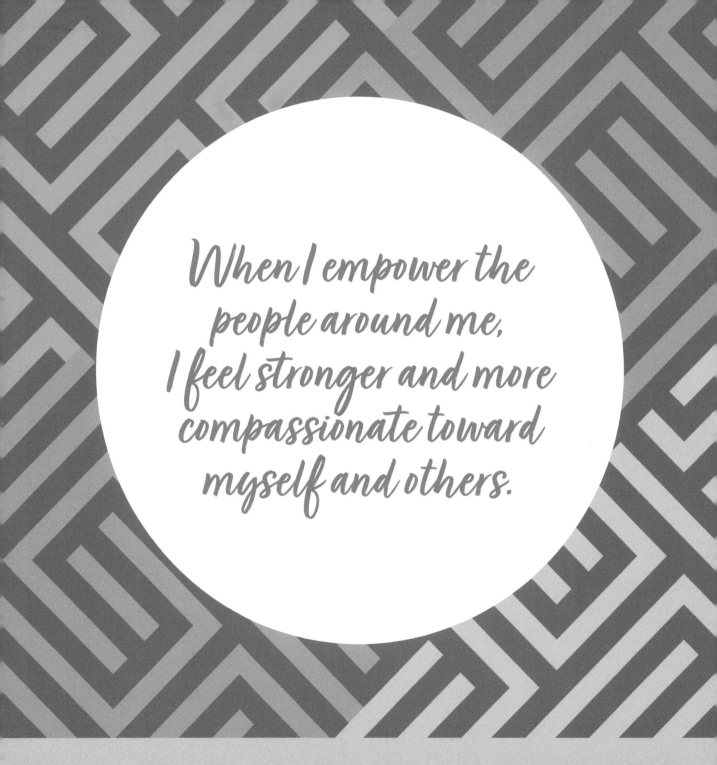

When I empower the people around me, I feel stronger and more compassionate toward myself and others.

How do you feel when someone says something kind or shares encouraging feedback? Do you feel inspired? Supported? Motivated? Make a list of the feelings that come up, remembering that this is how you can make others feel when you empower them.

_____

_____

_____

_____

_____

_____

_____

_____

_____

_____

_____

_____

_____

_____

_____

Simply living an empowered life can inspire others to do the same. What does it mean to you to be a source of inspiration? Do you see yourself as an inspiring person? Why or why not?

_____

_____

_____

_____

_____

_____

_____

_____

_____

_____

_____

_____

_____

_____

_____

_____

THE SEVEN-DAY STRANGER EMPOWERMENT CHALLENGE

DOESN'T IT FEEL GOOD when someone you don't know tells you they love your outfit or that you're doing a great job? You get to be that person for someone else—but not just someone you know. Empowering a total stranger allows you to touch the life of someone you may have otherwise walked by.

Empower one person you don't know every single day this week, whether it's someone you've never spoken to at school or in your office, or someone you walk past.

- Day 1: Give someone a compliment.

- Day 2: Recognize someone's hard work.

- Day 3: Offer someone advice.

- Day 4: Encourage someone who's struggling.

- Day 5: Ask for advice from someone (everyone wants to feel their opinions matter).

- Day 6: Give someone your time.

- Day 7: Cheer someone up.

In an increasingly online world, positivity is powerful. List at least three ways you can empower your online communities and choose one to do this week. A simple act of encouragement and positivity online can go a long way.

_____

_____

_____

_____

_____

_____

_____

_____

_____

_____

_____

_____

_____

_____

_____

_____

What are the characteristics of a great leader in your opinion? List as many as you can think of. Then, ask yourself, *Do I embody these characteristics? If not, how can I embrace them to lead and empower the people in my life?*

_____

_____

_____

_____

_____

_____

_____

_____

_____

_____

_____

_____

_____

_____

_____

_____

_____

_____

FINDING YOUR EMPOWERMENT
ZONE OF GENIUS

There are so many ways to empower others. Which ones do you feel most confident doing? When you know how you can best help others, you can do more of it.

Identify one way you'll empower someone each day this week, using your confidence as a guide. For example, your Empowerment Zone of Genius might be leading at work, so your Empowerment To-Do is to give advice to an entry-level co-worker.

MY EMPOWERMENT ZONE OF GENIUS	MY EMPOWERMENT TO-DO

Changing the lives of others changes your life, too. Recall one time when empowering someone else made you feel empowered as well. What did you do? How did they react? How did that change the way you interact with others?

_____

_____

_____

_____

_____

_____

_____

_____

_____

_____

_____

_____

_____

_____

_____

_____

_____

EMPOWER OTHERS BY EXAMPLE

Who empowers you in your daily life? This person can be a source of inspiration as you look to share your strength and power with the people around you, too. What does she do to empower you and how can you do that for someone else?

_____

_____

_____

_____

_____

_____

_____

_____

_____

_____

_____

_____

_____

_____

_____

_____

_____

PRAISE OTHERS FOR HAVING WHAT YOU WANT

JEALOUSY AND COMPARISON STOP you from being your most empowered self. If a co-worker gets a raise and you don't, or your friend meets the love of her life and you're still looking, the immediate reaction may be jealousy.

Instead of letting that feeling take over, muster your strength to congratulate them. Visualize letting go of that negative energy and you might feel a sigh of relief. List three people who have something you desire and how you'll get in touch. When you reach out, use this as an opportunity to share how proud of or happy you are for them.

I will congratulate Person 1: _____

for: _____

by form of contact: _____

I will congratulate Person 2: _____

for: _____

by form of contact: _____

I will congratulate Person 3: _____

for _____

by form of contact: _____

How has being empowered changed your life? Think back to a time when a teacher, friend, or relative encouraged you in some way. How did that encouragement impact you? Did you achieve something you would have otherwise struggled to accomplish?

_____

_____

_____

_____

_____

_____

_____

_____

_____

_____

_____

_____

_____

_____

_____

_____

Think of one person you'd like to empower. Perhaps a friend is struggling, or your sibling doesn't see their own strength. List three ways you can empower that person this week and make a plan for doing each one.

_____

_____

_____

_____

_____

_____

_____

_____

_____

_____

_____

_____

_____

_____

_____

_____

_____

_____

INSPIRE BY SIMPLY BEING

You can empower others simply by living an empowering life. When you do, you model those behaviors, ways of being, and actions to everyone around you. Although you may already do this unconsciously, getting intentional about how you empower yourself can encourage others to make even more empowering choices, too.

What three ways can you empower yourself and others this week? For example, you can choose a healthy lunch when everyone else is getting a burger. When others see you make this choice, they're inspired to take care of themselves, too.

I will empower myself and others by _____

_____

_____.

I will empower myself and others by _____

_____

_____.

I will empower myself and others by _____

_____

_____.

What negative beliefs are stopping you from empowering others right now? Do you feel there's not enough to go around or that you're not enough of a leader? Make a list and then replace each negative belief with a positive one. For example, "I am a leader in my own unique way."

_____

_____

_____

_____

_____

_____

_____

_____

_____

_____

_____

_____

_____

_____

_____

How can you use the strength of your voice to empower others? Can you speak up for someone or something that you've stayed silent about?

LET GO OF YOUR OPINIONS
TO LET OTHERS SOAR

You can easily disempower someone by pushing your own opinions and judgments on them. For example, if a friend is excited about a new project that you don't think is good, you can quickly deflate her enthusiasm by saying, "Interesting, I wouldn't do that . . ." rather than saying, "Wow, good for you!"

Your job is to empower others, not to be right or put your opinion on them when they're not asking for it. See how many of the following supportive, nonjudgmental words and phrases you can use this week (your challenge is to use at least three!) and check them off as you go.

☐ Congratulations!

☐ Sounds awesome!

☐ You got this.

☐ I'm cheering you on!

☐ Way to go!

☐ Let me know how it goes!

☐ Let me know how I can help.

☐ Brilliant!

☐ Look at you go!

☐ You're doing great.

☐ I'm proud of you!

It's often the smallest actions that make the biggest difference in the lives of those around you. What small actions can you take to empower people you see every day? Think of things you can say or do that may seem insignificant but can have a powerful impact.

_____

_____

_____

_____

_____

_____

_____

_____

_____

_____

_____

_____

_____

_____

_____

_____

What makes you a strong person who's capable of empowering others? List at least ten powerful qualities you possess (toot your own horn!), and then claim them as yours. Owning all that you are is just one way of empowering others to do the same.

_____

_____

_____

_____

_____

_____

_____

_____

_____

_____

_____

_____

_____

_____

_____

YOUR EMPOWERMENT WRAP-UP

Empowering others often leads to greater long-term happiness while also making you feel stronger and more connected to the people around you. Use this exercise to recap what you've done to empower others and how you're feeling as a result.

Use the following prompts to look back on all the empowering shifts you've made. You may be surprised by how good you feel when you take a moment to reflect.

When I empower others, I feel . . .

_____

_____

_____

_____

The most rewarding experience of empowering someone else was . . .

_____

_____

_____

_____

Three words that describe my experience of empowering others are . . .

_____

_____

_____

_____

_____

_____

I will continue empowering others by . . .

_____

_____

_____

_____

_____

_____

_____

EMPOWER OTHERS BY EXAMPLE

Her success is my success, and together we share in that joy.

A FINAL NOTE

You've come so far since you picked up this journal and decided to become a stronger woman—go pat yourself on the back; you did some really hard work! Don't forget to continue building your strength—it needs to be continually flexed and tested so it's always there when you reach for it. These exercises, practices, affirmations, and journal prompts can be used over and over to do exactly that, so keep them close, keep pushing yourself, and don't forget: Your strength is as unique as you. Own it, claim it, and make it your own!

RESOURCES

PODCAST

Building Psychological Strength by April Seifert, PhD. Pairs her knowledge with practical ideas and strategies so you can become a stronger woman.

BOOK

Grit: The Power of Passion and Perseverance by Angela Duckworth. Explains why grit is so important and how it can impact your life.

BLOG

Innovative Tools and Practical Advice to Create a Life You Love Living by the Brave Thinking Institute. Topics range from being a stronger leader to taking care of your mental health. With fresh content posted regularly, there's something for everyone.

APP

Moodfit. An important part of building your strength is doing the daily work of checking in with your feelings, thoughts, and emotions, and this app makes it easier than ever to do exactly that.

ACKNOWLEDGMENTS

I can't finish this book without thanking the people who have made me the strong woman that I am today.

To my mother, you were teaching me how to be strong before I ever knew what being strong meant. You've always been a pillar of strength, through good times and bad, and I wouldn't be writing this book if it weren't for you.

To my husband, Ben, you help me see my strength and power every single day, especially on the days when I don't see it myself. There are no words to adequately express my gratitude for our partnership and love.

To the incredible women in my family, my aunts, my grandmother, and my mother-in-law, you are all role models of strength and vulnerability, and I am so blessed to call you my family.

To my best girlfriends, you lift me up and cheer me on every single day. Together we've learned how to be strong, advocate for ourselves, and grow into the powerful women that we are today. Having you by my side is an honor.

ABOUT THE AUTHOR

Jessica Thiefels is a CEO, podcast host, and author whose mission is empowering women to make their own rules and live with intention.